Tsunamis

D0125947

Tsunamis

PORTER COUNTY LIBRARY

Margaret W. Carruthers

Kouts Public Library
101 E. Daumer Road
Kouts, IN 46347

Watts LIBRARY™

NOV 0 1 2005

Franklin Watts
A Division of Scholastic Inc.
New York • Toronto • London • Auckland • Sydney
Mexico City • New Delhi • Hong Kong
Danbury, Connecticut

J NF   551.4637 CAR   KO
Carruthers, Margaret W.
Tsunamis /
33410008575229

For Richard

Note to readers: Definitions for words in **bold** can be found in the Glossary at the back of this book.

Photographs © 2005: AP/Wide World Photos: 9 (Gemunu Amarasinghe), cover (APTN), 5 bottom, 34 (Katsumi Kasahara), 44 (Andres Leighton); Corbis Images: 48 (Patrick M. Bonafede/U.S. Navy), 8 (Kin Cheung/Reuters), 21 (Lloyd Cluff), 14 (Bob Krist), 42 (Yuriko Nakao/Reuters), 33 (Douglas Peebles), 5 top, 10 (Reuters), 39 (Galen Rowell), 26 (Royalty-Free), 13 (Randy Wells), 30; Getty Images: 2 (AFP), 16 (Ezquiel Becerra/AFP), 40 (Nat Farbman/Time Life Pictures), 50 (NOAA/AFP), 6 (John Russell/AFP); International Tsunami Information Center/A. Yamauchi/Honolulu Star-Bulletin: 32; Library of Congress: 22; Pacific Tsunami Museum: 36; Peter Arnold Inc./Otto Stadler: 43; Photo Researchers, NY/SPL: 38; U.S. National Oceanic & Atmospheric Adminstration (NOAA) and U.S. National Tsunami Hazard Mitigation Hazard: 28, 46; USGS.gov/Eric Geist: 25.

Illustrations by Bob Italiano

The photograph on the cover shows a still video image of the tsunami coming ashore at Thailand's Phuket resort on December 26, 2004. The photograph opposite the title page shows tourists reacting as the first of six tsunamis roll toward a beach near Krabi, Thailand, on the same day.

Library of Congress Cataloging-in-Publication Data

Carruthers, Margaret W.
 Tsunamis / Margaret W. Carruthers.
  p. cm. — (Watts library)
 Includes bibliographical references and index.
 ISBN 0-531-12286-7
 1. Tsunamis—Juvenile literature. I. Title. II. Series.
 GC221.5.C37 2005
 551.46'37—dc22   2005001467

© 2005 Margaret W. Carruthers.
All rights reserved. Published simultaneously in Canada.
Printed in the United States of America.
1 2 3 4 5 6 7 8 9 10 R 14 13 12 11 10 09 08 07 06 05

Contents

On December 26, 2004, people flee as a tsunami wave crashes ashore at Koh Raya in southern Thailand. The photographer escaped injury.

Indian Ocean, 2004

It was the morning of December 26, 2004, and ten-year-old British schoolgirl Tilly Smith was playing on Maikhoa beach on the island of Phuket, Thailand. She and her family were spending Christmas vacation there.

At about 9:45 A.M., something very strange happened to the sea. The water appeared to drain back into the Indian Ocean. Tourists watched in amazement as the water disappeared and boats were left stranded on the seafloor. Remembering

Silent "T"

The word *tsunami* is pronounced soo-NAH-mee.

a recent geography lesson about **tsunamis,** Tilly recognized with horror what was going on. She rushed over to warn her parents. She and her parents then alerted the staff at the hotel and everyone on the beach. The tourists evacuated the beach and retreated to the upper floors of the hotel. Minutes later, just as Tilly had predicted, the sea came rushing back in. It flooded the beach, ripped trees from the ground, and surrounded the hotel.

It had all begun some two hours earlier and 350 miles (560 kilometers) away, off the coast of Sumatra, Indonesia. Just before 7:59 A.M. local time, a mass of rock more than 15 miles (24 km) beneath the seafloor began to tear. As the crust ruptured and the rocks shifted, a powerful **earthquake** shook the

A debris-strewn resort near the popular Patong beach in Phuket, Thailand, three days after the Indian Ocean tsunami slammed the coast.

region for three minutes. The shifting seafloor jolted the ocean itself, setting off a chain of enormous **water waves** that raced out in all directions. It was a tsunami.

Fifteen minutes later, the waves struck the Indonesian island of Sumatra, destroying villages and carrying debris as high as 115 feet (35 meters) and as far as 4 miles (6 km) inland. By the end of the day, waves had hit Thailand, Sri Lanka, India, Somalia, Kenya, Tanzania, South Africa, and Madagascar.

The 2004 Indian Ocean tsunami ravaged the shores of several countries. Here, tsunami waves wash through houses in a Sri Lankan village.

All along the coasts of the Indian Ocean, people had no warning. Some, like the tourists at Maikhoa beach, were lucky. When they saw the water rushing in, they were able to run up hills, climb tress, and scramble on top of buildings. Many others were not. Some drowned. Some were battered against rocks. Some were struck by broken boards or squashed between buildings and trees ripped up by the waves. More than 5,000 people in Thailand, 10,000 in India, and 38,000 in Sri Lanka died. And in Indonesia, the country closest to the earthquake, the giant waves killed more than 170,000 people. The December 26 tsunami was the deadliest in human history.

Tsunamis in shallow water are powerful, as shown in this still from an amateur video taken in Penang, Malaysia.

Chapter One

Making Waves

A tsunami is a series of very long, very fast waves that form without warning when something disturbs the ocean. Out in the deep ocean, tsunamis are fast, small, silent, invisible, and harmless. As they travel toward the shore into shallow water, they slow down and become higher, steeper, and extremely dangerous.

Tsunamis don't occur very often. On average, about five tsunamis are recorded every year, and only one of those is destructive. Some tsunamis affect just one or two places close to where they form. Others travel vast distances in many directions, drowning cities and sweeping away villages that are thousands of miles apart on opposite sides of the ocean. Over the past 150 years, tsunamis have killed more than 350,000 people.

Waves Created by Wind

Most of the waves we see moving ocean water up and down, or crashing on the shore, form when wind blows across the water. Wind waves tend to be relatively small. The longest are only a few hundred yards from **wave crest** to wave crest, and most are no higher than about 10 feet (3 m). Occasionally, ferocious storms can whip up waves as high as 100 feet (30 m).

A wavelength is the distance between two successive wave crests.

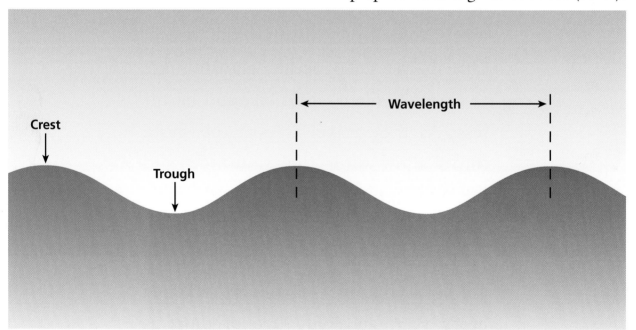

These ocean waves are created by wind. The surface of the sea appears choppy, but the water deep down is calm.

Although they look powerful, wind waves usually affect only the surface of the ocean, not the whole **water column** (the ocean from the surface down to the seafloor). Even when the weather is bad and the surface of the ocean is very choppy, the water down deep is calm. During the roughest storms, a submarine has to dive only 500 feet (150 km) or so for a smooth ride.

Waves Created by Moon and Earth

If you have ever spent more than a few hours on the coast, you have probably noticed another kind of wave. Over a period of about six hours, the ocean level slowly rises. If you are at the beach, you will notice the water slowly creep up farther on the sand. If you are at a harbor, you will see the water getting deeper. It gets to its highest point and then slowly falls. After

Tidal Wave!

If you've spent any time at the ocean, you've seen a tidal wave. Contrary to popular belief, tidal waves and tsunamis are not the same thing. Tidal waves are simply **tides**.

The maximum water level of the ocean is called high tide. The minimum level is low tide, shown here on Folly Beach, South Carolina.

a few more hours, the water will reach its lowest point and then start rising again. This rise and fall is part of Earth's natural cycles. It happens over and over, day after day, regardless of weather or season.

This continuous rise and fall of the ocean water is actually a series of enormously long waves called tides. Tides are so long that they stretch from one side of Earth to the other. The time between the highest and lowest tides lasts a little more than twelve hours. Tides don't look a lot like wind waves. In most places on Earth, they rise slowly up the beach, instead of crashing dramatically on the shore.

Tides are created by the gravitational attraction between Earth and the Moon and Sun. Because the Moon and Sun pull on the entire ocean, not just its surface, tides affect the entire ocean system. Because they are so predictable, tides aren't very dangerous.

Tsunami Waves

A tsunami is an entirely different sort of wave. Neither the weather nor the position of the Earth, Moon, and Sun causes tsunamis. Tsunamis form when some force suddenly shifts massive amounts of water. That force could be an earthquake, a volcanic eruption, a landslide, an asteroid impact, or even an explosion.

From the side, a tsunami looks like any other wave you might see in water—like an elongated S on its side. If you could view a tsunami from high above the ocean, it would look like a bull's-eye pattern of waves speeding out from a central point or groups of parallel waves moving in opposite directions.

Tsunamis are longer, faster, and much more powerful than wind waves. In the deep sea, tsunamis can be up to 650 miles (1,050 km) long and only a few inches high, speeding through the ocean at 500 miles (800 km) per hour. That's as fast as a jetliner. When they hit land, they can rise tens of stories high, flooding several miles inland.

Like tides, tsunamis affect the entire water column of the ocean, from the surface to the seafloor. However, they have a shorter **wave period** than tides—between about ten minutes and an hour—which means that they can flood the coast much more quickly. And unlike tides, they are extremely unpredictable.

Residents of this seaside village walk past the rubble following the earthquake-caused tsunamis that devastated a large stretch of Nicaragua's coast in 1992.

Chapter Two

What Causes Tsunamis

Most tsunamis are caused by strong earthquakes beneath the seafloor. An earthquake occurs when a mass of rock breaks and the pieces then move against one another along a surface called a **fault.** In some cases, the rocks slide past each other horizontally. In others, one mass of rock is forced upward, while another drops down. Huge sections of the ocean floor can move during an earthquake, pushing some of the ocean water up and sucking some of it down.

Earthquakes take place every day. Only some can move the ocean floor enough to create giant waves. To generate a tsunami, an earthquake must be very powerful—usually 7.5 or higher on the **Richter scale.** The Richter scale is the way scientists describe earthquakes based on how strong they are. A **magnitude** 7 earthquake, for example, generally releases thirty times more energy than a magnitude 6 earthquake.

On average, about twenty earthquakes of magnitude 7 or greater occur every year. Earthquakes of magnitude 8 or greater occur once or twice a year. However, many of these quakes take place on land or are too deep—more than 30 miles (50 km) beneath the ocean floor—to generate a tsunami. The great San Francisco earthquake of 1906 had a magnitude of about 7.8 on the Richter scale. It created only a mini-tsunami just a few inches high in the San Francisco Bay. The earthquake tore Earth's crust beneath the bay, but most of the rock moved back and forth rather than up and down, so the water in the bay wasn't moved enough to form a large tsunami.

In general, the higher the Richter magnitude, the more seafloor an earthquake disrupts and the larger the tsunami it creates. However, this isn't always the case. On the evening of September 1, 1992, a magnitude 7 earthquake struck off the Pacific coast of Nicaragua. People in Central America are used to earthquakes, and this one was just a low, soft rumbling that hardly seemed to shake the region. Many people didn't even feel the earthquake. However, a few minutes later, waves measuring between 10 and 30 feet (3 to 10 m) destroyed twenty-six

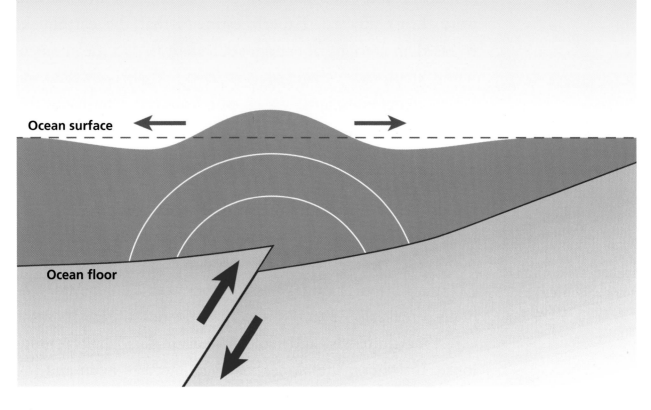

Ocean surface

Ocean floor

towns along the coast of Nicaragua and killed more than 150 people. Scientists determined that the earthquake had moved an area of seafloor 120 miles (200 km) long and 60 miles (100 km) wide, a lot more than anyone thought was possible. Nicaragua had been hit by what geologists now call a slow or silent earthquake.

The earthquake that caused the Indian Ocean tsunami of 2004 measured 9.0 on the Richter scale and was the most powerful earthquake in forty years. It ruptured a section of the ocean crust that was 750 miles (1,200 km) long and 60 miles (100 km) wide, and it moved the rocks about 50 feet

A diagram illustrates how powerful earthquakes beneath the ocean floor can cause tsunami waves.

(15 m) in just three minutes. Several yards of the seafloor were thrust upward. Experts estimate that the earthquake released an amount of energy equivalent to 475 megatons of TNT, an explosive material. An earthquake this powerful was bound to generate large waves. Fortunately, earthquakes this powerful are rare.

Landslides

Landslides are probably the second-most common cause of tsunamis. Parts of the ocean floor, especially near continents and ocean islands, are rugged, with steep slopes. Every so often, a huge mass of rock, sand, and mud suddenly breaks loose and slides into deeper water. In some cases, earthquakes and volcanic eruptions shake things loose; in others, the slopes just become too steep and the sediments get too heavy. As the material slides, it sucks down the water above and behind it, and pushes the water ahead of it. If the slide is big enough and fast enough, it can create a tsunami.

It was a rockfall that generated the highest waves ever witnessed by humankind. On July 9, 1958, a strong earthquake shook the coastal mountains of southeast Alaska. Two minutes later, an enormous mass of rock broke loose from a steep cliff along Lituya Bay and plunged into the water. With a deafening splash, a wave rose up, raced across the bay, and smashed into the opposite shore 1,700 feet (520 m) high. That's 250 feet (75 m) higher than the Empire State

A Megaton of TNT

A megaton is equal to 1 million tons (907,000 metric tons). The amount of energy that is given off when just one megaton of TNT explodes is enough to power more than 10 billion 100-watt lightbulbs for an hour.

Building. A wave at least 100 feet (30 m) high then roared toward the mouth of the bay at 100 miles (160 km) an hour. When it reached the shores, the wave leveled the forest, stripped the bark from the trees, and washed the soil from the rock.

Volcanic Eruptions

On the evening of August 27, 1883, the volcanic island of Krakatoa began to erupt. At first, the waves that washed up

The Lituya Monster

According to a legend of the Tlingit people of southeastern Alaska, Lituya Bay is inhabited by a giant monster, Kah Lituya. Kah Lituya detests visitors and enjoys overturning ships by shaking the bay with great waves.

In 1958, an earthquake in Alaska caused a large landslide that hit Lituya Bay, producing one of the largest tsunamis ever recorded. This photograph shows the bay fourteen years after the quake and resulting tsunami.

THE ISLAND AND VOLCANO OF KRAKATOA, STRAIT OF SUNDA, SUBMERGED DURING THE LATE ERUPTION.—[SEE PAGE 614.]

This wood engraving of the island and volcano of Krakatoa was published in Harper's Weekly *in 1883, soon after the volcano erupted, causing the deadly tsunami.*

on the nearby islands of Sumatra and Java were small enough to run away from. But as the eruption became more powerful, the waves grew larger, and by the next morning, 30-foot (10-m) waves had begun to destroy the villages along the coast. Then at about 10 A.M., Krakatoa blew itself to pieces, generating enormous waves that sped across the sea toward the distant shore. Waves 135 feet (40 m) high devoured 295 villages and killed nearly forty thousand people. When it was over, no witnesses were alive.

Volcanic eruptions can cause tsunamis in a number of ways. First of all, when a volcano erupts, massive amounts of volcanic lava and rock flow into the ocean or fly through the air and then fall into the ocean, making waves. Second,

22

when hot lava comes in contact with ocean water, it can heat the water up so quickly that the water explodes and creates a wave. Finally, after spewing a huge volume of material, a volcano can suddenly and catastrophically collapse in on itself. The ocean water above or surrounding the volcano gets sucked down, and waves **propagate** out in every direction. All of these things happened when Krakatoa erupted, and they all had a hand in generating one of the deadliest tsunamis in history.

Asteroid and Comet Impacts

Fortunately, no one has ever witnessed the effects of a giant rock plunging into the ocean. But there's not much doubt that it has happened in the past. Over the 4.5 billion years of its life, Earth has been hit by countless meteorites, from microscopic spheres to huge comets and giant asteroids hundreds of miles across.

Some 65 million years ago, an asteroid or comet more than 6 miles (10 km) across plummeted into a shallow sea in the area that is now the Yucatan Peninsula of Mexico. When it hit, an explosion as powerful as 100 million megatons of TNT carved a crater more than 60 miles (100 km) across out of the seafloor. It also created an enormous **megatsunami** that raced across the Gulf of Mexico and out into the rest of the ocean.

Geologists estimate that waves 150 to 300 feet (50 to 100 km) high flooded present-day Texas, Louisiana, Alabama, and

Florida as well as Mexico. The tsunami was so powerful that it probably collided with most of Earth's coastlines. Although no people were around to witness this event, we do have evidence for it. In Cuba, for example, the tsunami appears to have laid down a thick layer of rock made of a jumbled mixture of mud, sands, and broken rock fragments.

Since three-quarters of Earth is covered in water, chances are that when the next large asteroid or comet hits, it will fall into the ocean. Fortunately, an object as big as 6 miles (10 km) across is likely to hit Earth only every 100 million years or so. However, even a smaller object could cause problems. In fact, a single impact could lead to several tsunamis: the first when the rock hits the water; the second after all the debris that is thrown up in the air comes crashing back down into the water; a third when the crater walls slump in; and numerous others as the force of the impact causes underwater landslides and perhaps even earthquakes in other areas.

Unnatural Hazards

Once in a while, people accidentally cause tsunamis. In December 1917, a tsunami swamped the port of Halifax, Nova Scotia, after a ship carrying explosives crashed into another ship and exploded. In 1979, a tsunami along the coast of France seems to have formed when a runway under construction at the Nice International Airport collapsed into the Mediterranean Sea.

Sometimes it is very difficult to determine what caused a particular tsunami. Geologists are still arguing about what caused the tsunami that killed 2,200 people in Papua New Guinea on July 17, 1998. Some say it was the earthquake that occurred about 30 miles (50 km) off the coast. Others say that the tsunami was too big and that it arrived too late for the earthquake to have caused it. They think that the earthquake created underwater landslides, which caused the tsunami.

This computer simulation of the 1998 Papua New Guinea tsunami shows how pieces of the ocean floor shift during an earthquake and sometimes cause water to rise up in the form of giant waves (illustrated by the red spike).

These are wind waves. It's almost impossible to see a tsunami wave out in the deep ocean.

Chapter Three

From Sea to Shore

If you were on a ship in the middle of the ocean and a tsunami traveled past, what would happen? Would you be picked up by the wave and carried across the ocean at 450 miles (725 km) per hour and then slammed into the shore? Fortunately not. In fact, you probably wouldn't even notice the wave.

In the open ocean, tsunamis are almost impossible to see. They are only a few inches to a few feet in height. They are so long, hundreds of miles from crest to crest, that you wouldn't be able to see the entire wave at once. On the evening of June 15, 1896, fishermen from Sanriku, Japan, came home to find that their entire village had been destroyed. Their families had drowned, and their houses had been battered and swept away by a tsunami. They had been working out in deep water just 20 miles (32 km) away and never even felt the deadly wave pass beneath them.

Even if the waves out at sea were steeper, tsunamis couldn't carry you very far. Although the waves move far and fast, the water does not. Water waves, whether they are wind waves, tidal waves, or tsunamis, are not made of water—they are

This model simulation of the Pacific-wide tsunami generated by the 1996 Andreanov Island earthquake is part of research about the early detection and forecast of tsunamis.

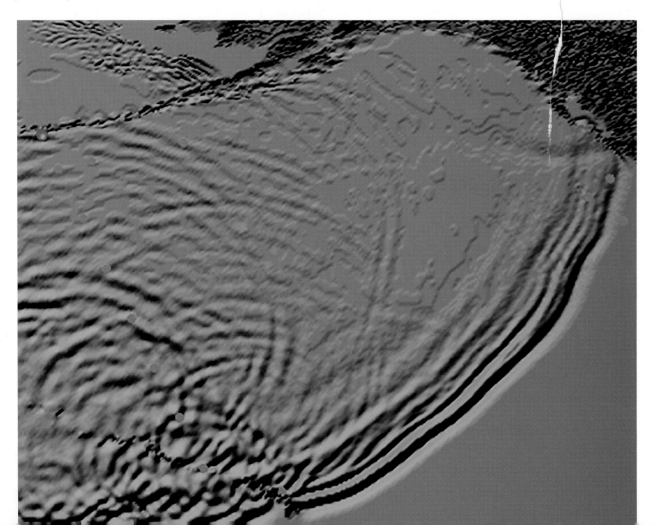

made of energy. Waves don't move water forward very much; they propagate forward *through* water.

Traveling Across the Ocean

In some cases, tsunamis don't travel very far from where they form, and they affect only nearby places. By the time they reach places far away, they have lost most of their energy. Waves that affect only the coastlines close to where they form are called **local tsunamis.**

Other tsunamis begin in one place and then move out in all directions, racing across the ocean at hundreds of miles per hour and maintaining their energy for thousands of miles. These tsunamis can affect hundreds of beaches, towns, and cities on all sides of the ocean. When a powerful earthquake shook the seafloor near the Kamchatka Peninsula of Russia in November 1952, it sent a tsunami all the way across the Pacific Ocean. Within a day, the waves had also hit Japan, Hong Kong, Micronesia, Papua New Guinea, the Solomon Islands, Kiribati, British Columbia, Mexico, Guatemala, El Salvador, Nicaragua, Costa Rica, Panama, Ecuador, Peru, Chile, New Zealand, Alaska, Hawaii, Washington, Oregon, and California. A tsunami of this sort is called an ocean-wide tsunami, or in this case, a **Pacific-wide tsunami.**

Coming Toward the Shore

A tsunami in the deep ocean is harmless. The trouble begins when it moves into shallow water. When a tsunami approaches the shore, several things happen: it slows down, its **wavelength** gets shorter, it gets much higher, and it therefore becomes much steeper.

The speed of a tsunami depends on two things: gravity and the depth of the water. Since gravity is almost exactly the same everywhere on Earth, the wave speed depends only on water depth. The deeper the water is, the faster the wave is. So when the waves move into shallow water, they slow down.

Because a single wave can be 100 miles (160 km) long, the front portion of the wave can be in shallow water while the back is still in the deep ocean. When this happens, the back part of the wave moves more quickly than the front. It begins to catch up with the front, and the wave gets shorter. The waves bunch up, getting higher and steeper as they approach

Many tsunami waves hit the shore like fast-moving tides. This tsunami wave washes over Laie Point on Oahu, Hawaii, in 1957.

land. A wave loses little energy as it moves onshore. As the distance between wave crests shortens, the energy becomes concentrated into less water and the tsunami becomes more powerful and much more dangerous.

Hitting the Shore

When most people think of a tsunami, they think of an enormous breaking wave, a wall of water that curls over the beach and then crashes, swallowing everything beneath it. Once in a while, along coasts with a steep near shore, tsunamis do behave this way. But in most cases, a tsunami isn't that steep when it hits the shore. Instead of crashing, it floods the land like a very fast-moving tide.

The depth of the water when the crest of the tsunami reaches the shore is called its **runup.** Runup depends only on the height of the wave when it hits land. The amount of land the wave actually floods is called **inundation.** Inundation depends on both the **wave height** and the shape of the land. A wave floods much less land where it runs up a steep cliff than where it runs up a flat beach.

Waves push water up and down, and at the beach this up-and-down movement looks like an in-and-out movement. In some cases, the first part of the wave to hit the shore is the **wave trough,** the lowest part of the wave.

This is what happened at Maikhoa beach in the Indian Ocean in 2004, when the water rushed out before it rushed in. If people know that they are seeing the trough of a tsunami,

The Wrap-Around Effect

The far sides of an island might seem safe from a tsunami, but in fact, this isn't true. When waves approach the shore, they can change direction, bend around a coast, and hit from almost any side.

they will have a few minutes to get to a safe place before the crest of the wave arrives. Unfortunately, many have no idea what's going to happen. Amazed by the sight of the disappearing ocean, unsuspecting people run down to inspect the dry seafloor. Instead of serving as a warning, this extraordinary event lures them to certain death.

The Wave Train

Another thing a lot of people don't know is that most tsunamis consist of more than one wave. This series of waves is called a wave train. The first wave is not necessarily the largest. Believing the tsunami has gone, people have returned to their houses and shops, only to be swept away by the second or third wave. It usually takes several hours for the water to settle down.

Between waves during the 1957 tsunami in Hawaii, residents inspect the seafloor and the stranded marine animals.

32

Large wind waves crash often on the shore. Because it is much longer and keeps moving, a tsunami wave is much more destructive.

The period between tsunami crests can be as little as ten minutes or as long as an hour. It's important to act quickly when you notice a tsunami because you might have only a couple of minutes between the time the water first starts rising above its normal level and the time the crest reaches the shore.

Death and Destruction

A 5-foot (1.5-m) wave doesn't seem as if it would be devastating. In fact, waves higher than that are generated by wind and crash on the shore all the time without hurting anyone. Normal waves break on the beach, and move water up and back down in a matter of seconds, without flooding very much of the shore.

A 5-foot (1.5-m) tsunami, however, is a completely different type of breaking wave. Once the crest of a tsunami wave arrives, the wave keeps moving onshore. A single wave can

Irregular Waves

Because coastlines and seafloors are irregular, tsunamis never affect two places in exactly the same way. In 1923, a tsunami that was 27 feet (8 m) high when it hit Suzaki, Japan, was only 2 feet (60 centimeters) high when it hit Toba, on the same coast 30 miles (50 km) away.

A tsunami can devastate coastal areas. A small fishing boat and a van are left overturned after a major earthquake in Japan shook Okushiri Island and a tsunami flattened the area in 1993.

flood the coast for thirty minutes. With miles of water behind it, its power is more like that of a deep, swift river.

A strong tsunami can flood vast areas of land, drowning people and animals and tearing apart buildings and trees. It can remove soil and rock from one place and deposit it in another, reshaping the landscape in minutes. Once the rushing water has picked up sand, mud, houses, trees, cars, and people, the water becomes more destructive. Many people are killed not by the water but by objects in the water that become battering rams. The trough of a tsunami can be as destructive as the crest. When the water rushes out, the currents can move as fast as 60 miles (100 km) per hour. They have the power to erode great gullies, rip buildings from the ground, and carry people far out to sea.

Like other natural disasters, tsunamis can have long-term effects as well. The flood can sever gas and electrical lines. Broken gas lines can start massive fires. With no passable roads, sanitation facilities, power, or supplies, tsunami survivors succumb to diseases such as cholera and gangrene. If a tsunami hits a business district, it could take years for the city to recover financially. Losses can be so great that certain communities never recover.

Tsunamis can have serious effects on the environment as well. Like hurricane waves, tsunami waves can reshape the coastline. Dry land becomes seafloor, and seafloor becomes dry land. Salty ocean water poisons freshwater ponds, affecting plant and animal life in the area. For people, the environmental effects can be devastating. Salt water contaminates fresh drinking water. Farmland flooded by ocean water can turn infertile for many years.

A Great Eruption

Around 1500 B.C., the volcanic island of Santorini erupted in the Aegean Sea. The eruption was so powerful that the island collapsed into the sea. The collapse created a tsunami that raced through the Mediterranean and battered cities all along the pathway. Historians estimate that as many as 100,000 people were killed. No one knows for sure, but many scientists think that the tsunami was part of the reason that the Minoan Civilization on the island of Crete died out.

The Pacific Ocean is a danger zone for earthquakes and volcanic eruptions—and the resulting tsunamis.

Chapter Four

Danger Zones

Tsunamis can form in any ocean, sea, or lake. They can flood any coastline in any part of the world. However, they occur more often in certain places.

Most tsunamis occur on the coasts of the Pacific Ocean. There are several reasons for this. First of all, the Pacific is the largest ocean in the world, and it has the longest coastline in the world—about 100,000 miles (160,000 km). Second, and more important, more earthquakes and volcanic eruptions occur in the Pacific than in any other ocean.

Tectonic Plates

The outermost layer of Earth is composed of about a dozen pieces called **tectonic plates.** The plates are interlocked like pieces of a jigsaw puzzle. Over time, the plates move, changing the positions of the continents and the sizes of ocean basins. The movement of these plates is what causes most earthquakes and many of the volcanic eruptions on Earth.

Most of the action takes place where the plates move against each other. There are three types of plate boundaries: divergent, transform, and convergent boundaries. At a **divergent boundary**, two plates move away from each other. A lot of small earthquakes and small volcanic eruptions occur at divergent boundaries. Very few are strong enough to create tsunamis.

The boundaries between the main tectonic plates on this projection of the Earth are marked in red. Most earthquakes and volcanic eruptions occur along these boundaries.

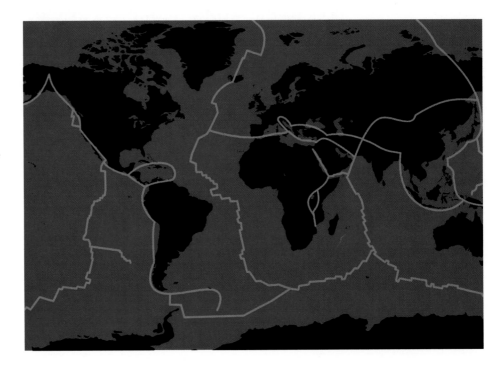

At a **transform boundary,** two plates scrape past one another. Many powerful earthquakes occur along transform boundaries. When they do move the seafloor, they usually move it back and forth rather than up and down. This can cause tsunamis, but most are not very powerful.

At a **convergent boundary,** two plates crash into each other, producing the most devastating earthquakes.

If both plates are composed of continents, they will deform, forming mountain chains such as the Himalayas. But if at least one is made of oceanic crust (seafloor), one plate will dive beneath the other. This type of plate boundary is also called a **subduction zone** because one plate descends beneath another.

The most powerful earthquakes and the most violent volcanic eruptions on Earth happen at subduction zones. So many tsunamis occur in the Pacific Ocean because it contains numerous subduction zones. The region is known as the "ring of fire" for its active volcanoes.

Mount Everest is part of the Himalayas, which began to form by the collision of two tectonic plates along a convergent boundary millions of years ago. They are still forming today.

California, Oregon, Washington, and British Columbia

Most of the tsunamis that have hit the west coast of the United States and Canada in historic times haven't been very destructive. The worst happened in 1964 when an

In 1964, a tsunami caused by an earthquake off the coast of Alaska piled up cars in Crescent City, California. The tsunami also took the lives of 112 people.

Its Name

When a wave moves from the open ocean into a narrow bay, its energy gets funneled into a smaller volume of water. Because of this fact, places like Hilo Bay, Hawaii, are particularly susceptible to high tsunami waves. Perhaps that's how tsunamis got their name: *tsunami* is Japanese for "harbor wave."

earthquake off the coast of Alaska sent a wave that ran up more than 20 feet (6 m) and killed 122 people, including 11 in Crescent City, California.

However, geologists think that the west coast is vulnerable to a devastating tsunami. The west coast of North America is also part of the ring of fire. There is a subduction zone off the coasts of Washington and British Columbia, and a series of explosive volcanoes in Oregon and Washington (the Cascades). In addition, a powerful transform fault lies in California (the San Andreas). And, of course, the coast is right across the ocean from Japan, Russia's Kamchatka Peninsula, and Alaska, where so many tsunamis originate.

Around the year 900, an earthquake shook Puget Sound on the coast of modern-day Washington and sent a tsunami crashing into what is now Seattle. Scientists studying the sand and mud left by the water, and computer simulations of the waves, estimate that the waves were 10 to 25 feet (3 to 8 m) high and flooded up to 1,000 feet (300 m) inland. If a wave of this magnitude happened today, it could affect several million people.

Hawaii and Other Pacific Islands

Hawaii is thousands of miles from the nearest subduction zone. But its location in the middle of the Pacific Ocean means it can be hit by tsunamis created almost anywhere in the Pacific. However, because it is so far from the major earthquake and volcanic zones where tsunamis form, it usually has several hours to prepare for the waves.

Many other Pacific islands are protected from tsunamis by coral reefs. Reefs are so steep that when a wave hits, it just bounces off and travels back to the ocean, without running up onto the land.

The Indian Ocean

Only two tsunamis in history have affected the whole of the Indian Ocean. However, these were two of the worst: the Krakatoan tsunami of 1883 and the Indonesian tsunami of 2004. There have also been numerous local tsunamis in Indonesia.

Almost all of the tsunamis in the Indian Ocean are caused by the Indian plate descending beneath the Asian plate. Because Indonesia lies right above this subduction zone, it is

An aerial photograph taken on January 6, 2005, shows damages caused by the Indian Ocean tsunami in Banda Aceh, Indonesia. Only one other tsunami in history has affected the entire Indian Ocean—the Krakatoan tsunami of 1883.

one of the most geologically active places on Earth. There are seventy-six active volcanoes in the islands, and earthquakes occur there nearly every day.

The Mediterranean and the Caribbean

The Mediterranean Sea is another place where a lot of earthquakes and volcanic eruptions occur. In fact, most of the tsunamis recorded in ancient times occurred in the Mediterranean. That's because this was the home of the people whose history we are most familiar with—the Greeks and the Romans.

The Caribbean is also at risk because there is a subduction zone and an arc of explosive volcanoes. A tsunami that originates in the Caribbean could hit not only those islands, but the northern coast of South America, the eastern coast of Central America, and the southern coast of the United States.

The Atlantic Coasts

There haven't been very many tsunamis in the Atlantic Ocean. There are no subduction zones on either side of the North Atlantic, and the volcanoes in the Atlantic are not particularly explosive. However, in 2001, a group of scientists warned that the Atlantic coasts of the United States, Europe, Central America, South America, and Africa are all at risk of being flooded by waves perhaps 150 feet (50 m) high. The cause would be the collapse of La Palma, a volcanic island in the Canary Islands off the coast of Morocco. The scientists claimed that if the volcano on La Palma erupted, it could dislodge a 120-cubic-mile (500-cubic-kilometer) mass of rock and mud that could then crash down the slopes below the water at about 560 miles (350 km) per hour.

There is a lot of evidence that massive landslides have occurred on La Palma in the past. But many scientists are not convinced that a landslide, even one this big, could actually move enough water to generate a wave powerful enough to reach the other side of the ocean.

How Many?

National Geophysical Data Center's Tsunami Database listed more than six thousand tsunamis in the last four thousand years!

Some scientists warn that the eruption of La Palma, a volcanic island in the Canary Islands, could cause a tsunami on the Atlantic coasts.

A sign in San Juan, Puerto Rico, warns passersby of a tsunami danger zone.

ZONA DE PELIGRO
MAREMOTO/TSUNAMI

EN CASO DE TERREMOTO
MUEVASE A UN LUGAR ALTO
O ALEJESE DE LA COSTA

CALL
SIN
SALID

Chapter Five

Preparing for the Future

At 2 A.M. on April 1, 1946, a powerful earthquake 2,300 miles (3,700 km) away shook the Aleutian Islands of Alaska. Five hours later, 30-foot (10-m) waves drowned the coasts of Hawaii, killing 159 people. Soon after the 1946 April Fool's Day tsunami, scientists and government officials began work on preventing such a tragedy from recurring. People had to be educated about the risks of tsunamis. Cities needed evacuation plans and warning signals. And because an event

The Deep-ocean Assessment and Reporting of Tsunamis (DART) system includes a seafloor bottom pressure recorder (lower left) and a moored surface buoy (center) for real-time communications to tsunami warning centers.

in one place can create a tsunami that hits every coast, the entire Pacific region needed to get together to form a tsunami tracking and warning system. In 1948, the Pacific Tsunami Warning System was created to detect and warn people about tsunamis along the Pacific Rim.

Tsunami Warnings

When an earthquake occurs, geologists quickly determine exactly where the earthquake occurred and how strong it was. If they think the strength and location of the event might generate a tsunami, they put out a message to tsunami warning centers around the world. They try to predict when and where a possible tsunami could hit. The warning centers then contact local governments, who tell residents living along the coast how to prepare for a possible tsunami. This system can give many people several hours' warning before a tsunami strikes.

Of course, not all tsunamis are generated by earthquakes, and not all strong earthquakes generate tsunamis. To detect a tsunami before it hits land, scientists use a **bottom pressure recorder (BPR).** A BPR

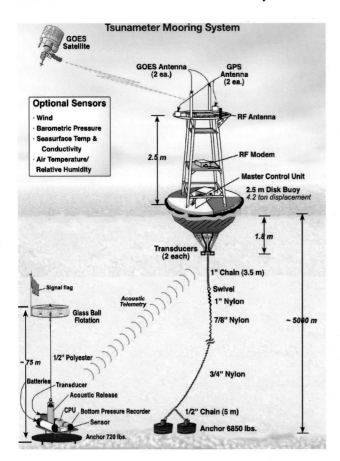

sits on the ocean floor and measures the weight of the water above it. If it detects a wave that is out of the ordinary, it transmits a signal to a buoy floating on the ocean. The buoy then sends the information to a satellite orbiting Earth, and the satellite relays the information to the tsunami warning centers.

Unfortunately, countries that lie along the Indian Ocean are not part of the Pacific Tsunami Warning System. When the earthquake occurred on December 26, 2004, the Pacific Tsunami Warning Center analyzed the information and came to the conclusion that there was no threat of a tsunami to the countries in the Pacific. There was no easy way to get information to the countries on the Indo-Rim. Even if there had been a way, by the time they were able to analyze the data completely, it was too late.

In the days following the 2004 tsunami, scientists and government officials all over the world began to recognize the importance of warning systems for every ocean. The United Nations plans to have a system for the Indian Ocean up and running by mid-2006. The plan is to improve education about tsunami hazards, to deploy more scientific equipment to detect tsunamis, and to establish a stronger network of systems to warn people throughout the world.

Studying Tsunamis

In order to warn the public, scientists need a better understanding of tsunamis. Because they are dangerous,

Interesting Test Signal
The tsunami warning test signal in Canon Beach, Oregon, is a long cow's "MOOOOOOO."

Because there weren't any tsunami warning systems in the Indian Ocean in 2004, most of the tsunami victims were taken by surprise. This view from the sky is of the decimated countryside near Banda Aceh, Indonesia.

unpredictable, and uncommon, tsunamis are extremely difficult to study.

Studying a tsunami in action is risky and challenging, but it can be done with a bit of planning. When a tsunami warning is issued in Hawaii, teams from the Tsunami Monitoring Program get to work. They set up cameras to film the waves. They set out BPRs to measure the height of the waves as they pass over. U.S. Navy patrol planes set out to fly in circles over the coast and photograph the waves as they come in. (Hawaii is a particularly good place to study tsunamis because they happen more often there than in most places; there are usually several hours to get ready; and there are safe places to observe them, high above the shore.)

After a tsunami hits, geologists collect a lot more information. After three enormous waves washed over a narrow sandbar and killed 2,200 people in Papua New Guinea in July 1998, an international team of scientists set out to investigate. They interviewed survivors, inspected the damage, measured how much land had been flooded, studied the sand, gravel, plant material, and erosion marks that the waves left behind, and estimated the wave crests. To help them determine the location and cause of the tsunami, they examined **seismograms** of earthquakes that occurred right before the tsunami and surveyed the seafloor for signs of landslides.

Scientists also study evidence of tsunamis from the distant past. Even places that have never experienced a tsunami in historic times can be at great risk. In Australia, shells and boulders of coral 70 to 100 feet (20 to 30 m) above sea level and several miles inland suggest possible tsunami activity in the past. On the east coast of Scotland, a layer of sediment may have been deposited by a tsunami caused by a landslide seven thousand years ago. Myths and legends also provide a lot of clues. Native American tribes living along the Pacific coast have many possible tsunami-related stories of the sea suddenly and mysteriously flooding the land.

A Red Sea Tsunami?

In the biblical story of the parting of the Red Sea, Moses led the Israelites out of Egypt toward the Promised Land. When they got to the sea, the water disappeared and they ran across the dry land to safety. As soon as they got to the other side, the water returned, drowning their pursuers.

Some scientists think that this story could be based on a true event—a tsunami. The trough of a tsunami could have drained the Red Sea. The people could have had as long as half an hour to get across a narrow part of the sea before the crest of the wave arrived and the sea returned.

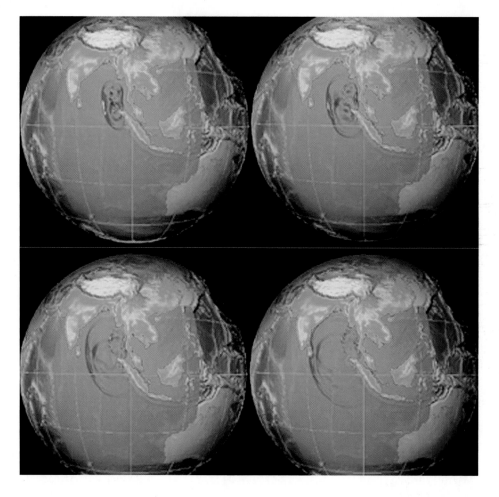

This illustration from the National Oceanic and Atmospheric Administration (NOAA) shows (clockwise from top left) the sequence of the tsunami caused by the massive Indonesian earthquake on December 26, 2004.

Scientists can also study tsunamis with physical models and computer programs. They can observe the waves changing shape as they approach the shore and determine which areas will get hit the hardest. They can input everything they know about the shape of the seafloor into a mathematical computer model and use the program to generate tsunamis of different strengths and locations to see how the waves travel. Computer simulations can also be used to figure out how and where the tsunami formed after it hits a coast.

Tsunami-Proofing

While no one can prevent a tsunami, it is possible to lessen its destruction. Planning ahead in tsunami-prone areas can be extremely valuable. After a tsunami hit Hilo Bay in 1960, residents decided to rebuild the city much farther from the ocean. A highway and a wide stretch of parkland now sit between the ocean and the city. Many of the larger hotels and businesses in Hawaii have their first floors high above ground level. The residents of Tarou, Japan, got so tired of being swamped by tsunamis that they built a wall 33 feet (10 m) tall and 4,500 feet (1,400 m) long to protect their town. Many other towns have decided to abandon the coastline and rebuild on higher ground after being destroyed by a tsunami.

Education

One of the most important things coastal communities must do is educate their residents and visitors. On March 28, 1964, when authorities in Crescent City, California, got the message that a tsunami was headed their way, they didn't even know what a tsunami was. Many people in the town went down to the seaside to watch it come in. They had no idea how big and how powerful the waves could be. Eleven people died that day, mainly because they didn't know enough about the danger.

During the Indian Ocean tsunami, thousands of lives could have been saved, even without an international warning system, if people simply had known what a tsunami was and how to recognize the warning signs, as Tilly Smith had.

Tsunamis are natural, unpreventable, and unstoppable. We still have a lot to learn about them. How exactly do they form? How can they be detected quickly and accurately—and all the time? What is the best way to educate and warn the public? And what path will the next tsunami take? Since the Indian Ocean tsunami of 2004, the world has never been more concerned about finding answers to these difficult questions.

Tsunami Warning Signs

At the beach, if you notice any of these signs, go to higher ground immediately. If there is no higher ground, climb a tree, get yourself on the roof of a tall building, or hold onto something that floats. Here are some signs that a tsunami may be approaching:

- You feel an earthquake. Even an earthquake that doesn't feel very powerful can create a tsunami.
- The sea rushes out, land that is usually underwater is dry, and sea animals are stranded.
- You hear a sound like a train or a jetliner coming from the ocean.

- A long, strange shadow is racing across the ocean toward the beach. The shadow is the wave.
- Someone familiar with the area notices that the sea or the beach looks strange. People are going down to the ocean to see what's happening. Do not follow them!
- A tsunami warning signal goes off or a warning is issued on the television or radio. Don't assume it's a false alarm, even if everyone else does.
- One or more waves have already come in. Tsunamis usually consist of several waves. Don't assume it's safe until several hours after the waves have struck.

Timeline

Around 1500 B.C.	The volcanic island of Santorini erupts in the Aegean Sea. Historians later estimate that as many as 100,000 people were killed.
Around A.D. 900	An earthquake shakes Puget Sound on what is now the coast of Washington and ends in a tsunami crashing into what is now Seattle.
1883	The volcanic island of Krakatoa in Indonesia erupts, causing tsunami waves that kill nearly forty thousand people.
1896	An earthquake-caused tsunami in Sanriku, Japan, kills some 26,000 people.
1946	A powerful earthquake shakes the Aleutian Islands of Alaska. Five hours later, waves drown the coasts of Hawaii, killing 159 people.
1948	The Pacific Tsunami Warning System is created to detect and warn people about tsunamis along the Pacific Rim.
1952	A powerful earthquake shakes the seafloor near Russia's Kamchatka Peninsula, causing a Pacific-wide tsunami that killed hundreds.
1964	A large earthquake off the coast of Alaska sends a tsunami wave that kills 122 people.
1992	A magnitude 7 earthquake off the Pacific coast of Nicaragua causes a tsunami that destroys twenty-six towns along the coast and kills more than 150 people.
1998	A tsunami kills 2,200 people in Papua New Guinea. Scientists disagree over the cause of the tsunami.
2004	On December 26, a magnitude 9.0 earthquake off the coast of Sumatra, Indonesia, causes a massive tsunami that strikes more than a dozen countries.
2005	One death toll of the 2004 tsunami reaches more than 280,000. An exact death toll may never be known.

Glossary

bottom pressure recorder (BPR)—an instrument that sits on the seafloor and detects waves by measuring the pressure of the water above it

convergent boundary—a place where two plates are moving toward one another

divergent boundary—a place where two plates are moving away from one another

earthquake—a shaking of the ground caused by large masses of rock breaking and moving against each other along a fault

fault—a plane along which large masses of rock move past one another

inundation—the distance inland that a tsunami floods

local tsunami—a tsunami that strikes coasts only within about 600 miles (1,000 km) of the related earthquake or landslide

magnitude (Richter magnitude)—a description of the strength of an earthquake as measured on the Richter scale

megatsunami—a tsunami with so much energy that it can travel to coastlines in many different parts of the world

Pacific-wide tsunami—a tsunami that strikes areas across the entire Pacific Ocean

propagate—to spread or extend

Richter scale—a system used to describe an earthquake's strength

runup—the vertical distance between average sea level and the highest point the tsunami reaches

seismogram—a record of earth tremors as measured by an instrument called a seismograph

subduction zone—a place where one plate descends beneath another; marked on Earth's surface by a deep ocean trench

tectonic plates—pieces of Earth's uppermost layer (the crust and the uppermost mantle), separated from other plates by large faults; there are about a dozen major plates

tides—the continuous rise and fall of the ocean water caused by the gravitational pull of the Moon and Sun

transform boundary—a place where two plates are sliding past each other

tsunami—a series of waves caused by earthquakes, volcanic eruptions, landslides, or meteorite impacts

water column—the ocean from water surface to the seafloor

water wave—a propagation of energy through water, which temporarily causes the water to move up and down

wave crest—the highest part of a wave

wave height—the vertical distance between the wave trough and the wave crest

wave period—the time it takes for an entire wavelength to pass a particular point

wave trough—the lowest point of a wave

To Find Out More

Books

Fredericks, Anthony D. *Tsunami Man: Learning About Killer Waves with Walter Dudley*. Honolulu: University of Hawai'i Press, 2002.

Kling, Andrew A. *Tsunamis*. San Diego: Lucent Books, 2002.

Thompson, Luke. *Tsunamis*. Danbury, CT: Children's Press, 2000.

Wade, Mary Dodson. *Tsunami: Monster Waves*. Berkeley Heights, NJ: Enslow Publishers, 2002.

Videos and DVDs

Killer Wave: Power of the Tsunami, National Geographic Video, 1997.

Tsunami: Wave of Destruction, ABC News/MPI Home Video, 2005.

Organizations and Online Sites

International Tsunami Information Center
http://www.prh.noaa.gov/itic/
Run by the United Nations Educational, Scientific, and Cultural Organization (UNESCO), this site provides current tsunami messages, recent and historical data, frequently asked questions, and safety rules.

National Geophysical Data Center's Tsunami Database
http://www.ngdc.noaa.gov/seg/hazard/tsu.shtml
On this site, you can search for details about more than six thousand tsunamis that have been recorded over the past four thousand years.

Pacific Tsunami Museum
130 Kamehameha Avenue
Hilo, HI 96721
http://www.tsunami.org/
This site provides information about tsunamis in Hawaii, a tsunami glossary, and tsunami stories and photographs as well as information about the museum.

U.S. National Tsunami Hazard Mitigation Program
http://www.pmel.noaa.gov/tsunami-hazard/tsunami_faqs.htm
This site answers frequently asked questions about tsunamis and provides related links.

University of Southern California Tsunami Research Group
http://www.usc.edu/dept/tsunamis/
This site includes an interactive world map of tsunamis, photos from field surveys, and computer simulations.

Tsunamis and Earthquakes at the U.S. Geological Survey
http://walrus.wr.usgs.gov/tsunami/index.html
This site includes tsunami computer animations, diagrams of the life of a tsunami, and links about surviving a tsunami.

A Note on Sources

I did all the research for this book using other books, research papers, photographs, and Web sites. The most useful books I found were *Tsunami!* by Walter Dudley and Min Lee and *The Great Waves* by Douglas Myles. I read journals such as the *Science of Tsunami Hazards*, abstracts from geological conferences, and Tsunami Info Alert newsletters. The National Tsunami Hazard Mitigation Program's Web site and the Web site of the University of Southern California's Tsunami Research Center gave me access to the most current information.

The best place to look for the latest, most accurate information about the Indian Ocean tsunami, and any other recent events, are Web sites run by research institutions. Be careful not to believe everything you read. It is generally best to use sources that have been published recently and written by experts in the field.

—*Margaret W. Carruthers*

Index

Numbers in *italics* indicate illustrations.

About the Author

Margaret W. Carruthers is the author of several science books for children and young adults, including *Pioneers of Geology: Discovering Earth's Secrets; Land, Sea and Air; and The Moon.* After receiving her bachelor of science degree in natural resources from the University of the South and master's degree in geology from the University of Massachusetts, Carruthers worked as a geologist and educator at the American Museum of Natural History in New York City. Since then, she has been writing, editing, and teaching. Carruthers, her husband, Richard Ash, and their dog, Sifa, live in Baltimore, Maryland, up on a hill far from subduction zones and volcanoes.